THE CANADIAN BRASS
15 FAVORITE HYMNS
TRUMPET DESCANTS

EASY TO INTERMEDIATE

ARRANGED BY LARRY MOORE

Note: These descants may be played with any standard hymnal. They are also compatible with *The Canadian Brass: 15 Favorite Hymns* for brass quartet or quintet.

Visit the official website of The Canadian Brass:
www.canbrass.com

HAL•LEONARD®
CORPORATION

7777 W. BLUEMOUND RD. P.O. BOX 13819 MILWAUKEE, WI 53213

Visit Hal Leonard Online at
www.halleonard.com

Trumpet Descant (B♭)
(optional)

CANADIAN BRASS

ALL CREATURES OF OUR GOD AND KING

LASST UNS ERFREUEN

Francis of Assisi
Trans. W.H. Draper

Geistliche Kirchengesang
Harmonized by Ralph Vaughan Williams

STANDARD VERSION
Joyously (♩ = 120)

Small notes are optional

Repeat as needed (opt.)

Amen

Trumpet Descant (B♭)
(optional)

CANADIAN BRASS

ALL GLORY, LAUD, AND HONOR

ST. THEODULPH

Theodulph of Orleans, ca. 820
Trans. by John Mason Neal, 1851; alt., 1859

Melchior Teschner, 1615

STANDARD VERSION
Regally (♩ = 108)

Trumpet Descant (B♭)
(optional)

CANADIAN BRASS
BLESSED ASSURANCE
ASSURANCE

Fanny J. Crosby

Phoebe P. Knapp

Trumpet Descant (B♭)
(optional)

CANADIAN BRASS

CHRIST THE LORD IS RISEN TODAY

Charles Wesley

EASTER HYMN

from *Lyra Davidica,* London, 1708

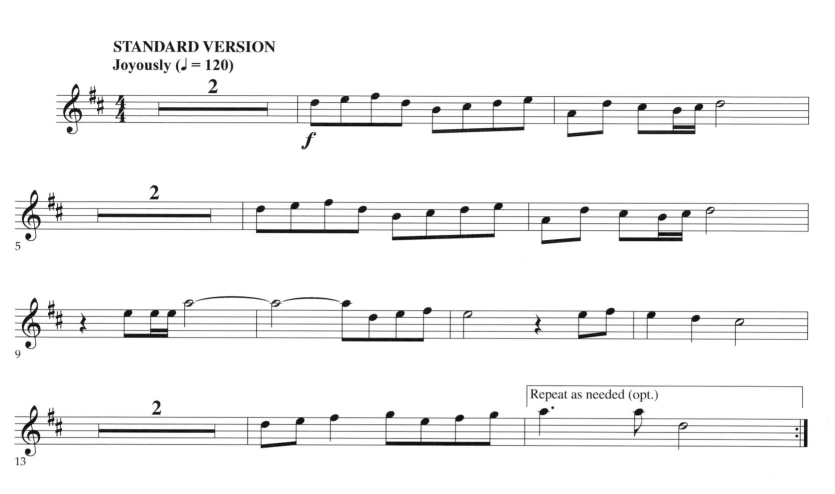

Trumpet Descant (B♭)
(optional)

CANADIAN BRASS

COME, YE THANKFUL PEOPLE, COME
ST. GEORGE'S, WINDSOR

Henry Alford

George J. Elvey

STANDARD VERSION
Regally (♩ = 120)

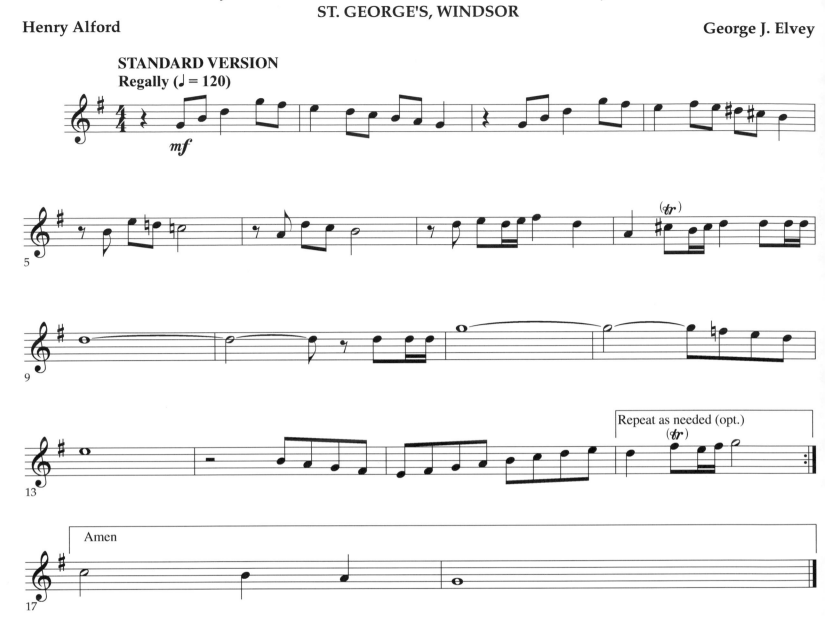

Trumpet Descant (B♭)
(optional)

CANADIAN BRASS
CROWN HIM WITH MANY CROWNS
DIADEMATA

Matthew Bridges, stanzas 1,2,4;
Godfrey Thring, stanza 3

George J. Elvey

Trumpet Descant (B♭)
(optional)

CANADIAN BRASS

FAIREST LORD JESUS
(Beautiful Savior)
CRUSADERS' HYMN

Anonymous German Hymn, *Munster Gesangbuch*, 1677;
translated, Source unknown, stanzas 1-3; Joseph A. Seiss, Stanza 4

Schlesische Volkslieder, 1842;
arranged by Richard S. Willis

Trumpet Descant (B♭)
(optional)

CANADIAN BRASS

FOR THE BEAUTY OF THE EARTH

DIX

Folliott S. Pierpoint, altered

Conrad Cocher;
arranged by William H. Monk

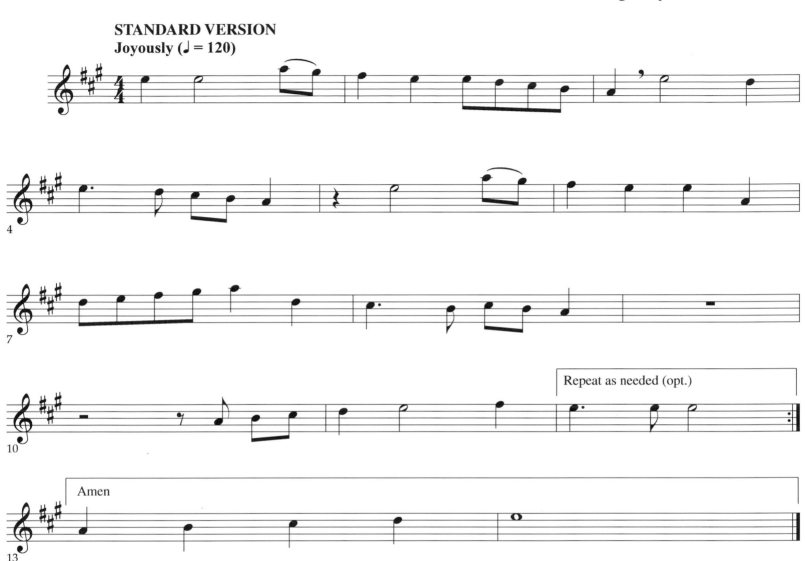

STANDARD VERSION
Joyously (♩ = 120)

Repeat as needed (opt.)

Amen

Trumpet Descant (B♭)
(optional)

CANADIAN BRASS
GOD OF OUR FATHERS
NATIONAL HYMN

Daniel C. Roberts

George W. Warren

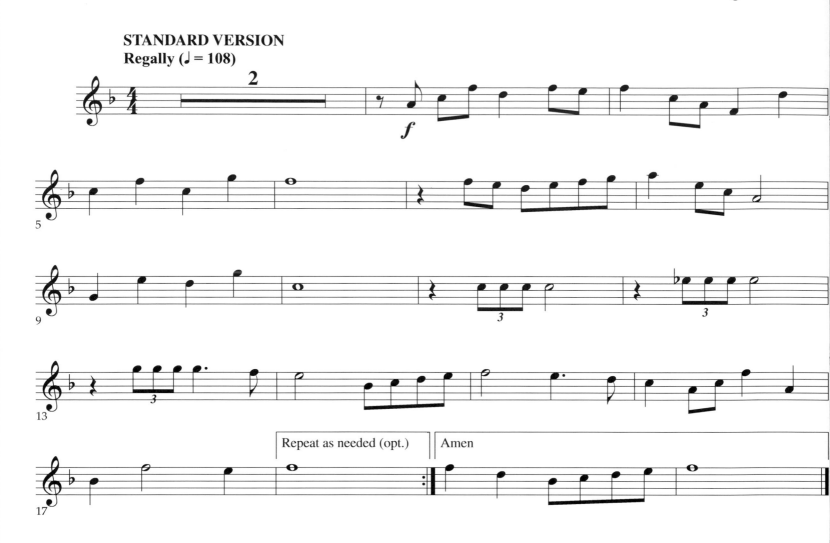

Repeat as needed (opt.)

Amen

CANADIAN BRASS

Trumpet Descant (B♭)
(optional)

GUIDE ME, O THOU GREAT JEHOVAH
(God of Grace and God of Glory)

CWM RHONDDA

William Williams;
translated by Peter Williams

John Hughes

STANDARD VERSION
Earnestly (♩ = 104)

Repeat as needed (opt.)   Amen

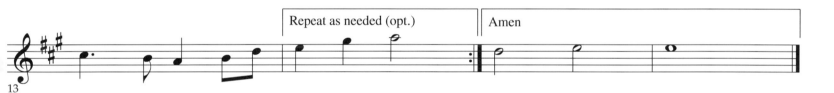

Trumpet Descant (B♭)
(optional)

CANADIAN BRASS
HOLY, HOLY, HOLY!
NICEA

Reginald Heber

John B. Dykes

STANDARD VERSION

Reverently (♩ = 80)

Trumpet Descant (B♭)
(optional)

CANADIAN BRASS

JOYFUL, JOYFUL, WE ADORE THEE
HYMN TO JOY

Henry van Dyke

Ludwig van Beethoven

STANDARD VERSION
Joyously (♩ = 132)

Trumpet Descant (B♭)
(optional)

CANADIAN BRASS
LEAD ON, O KING ETERNAL
LANCASHIRE

Ernest W. Shurtleff

Henry T. Smart

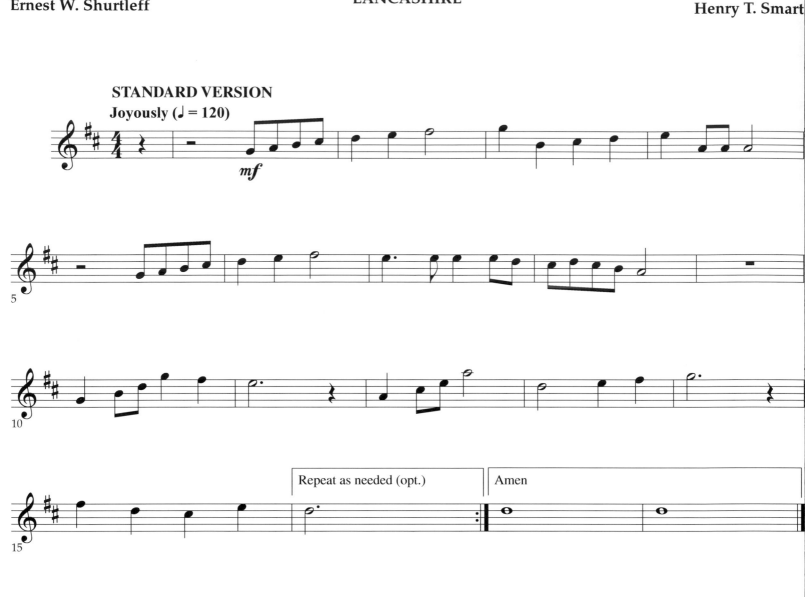

Trumpet Descant (B♭)
(optional)

CANADIAN BRASS

A MIGHTY FORTRESS IS OUR GOD

EIN FESTE BURG

Martin Luther
Trans. by F.H. Hedge, based on Psalm 46

Martin Luther

Trumpet Descant (B♭)
(optional)

CANADIAN BRASS

O GOD, OUR HELP IN AGES PAST

ST. ANNE

Isaac Watts;
based on Psalm 90

attr. William Croft